Love Baisant

Love Baisant
Cathy Watness

ISBN-13: 978-1-948712-86-6

© 2021 Cathy Watness

Red Ferret Press
an Imprint of Weasel Press
Lansing, MI
https://www.weaselpress.com/red-ferret-press

CONTENTS

Love Baisant

Cathy Watness

RED FERRET PRESS

The Vixen and the Snake

Once there was a vixen who found herself in love with a snake

Now you might ask
how can a vixen fall for a snake?
Many have been tricked by serpentine eyes and voice and heart
One would think a creature known for her cunning and skeptical
        nature
would have enough sense to avoid a snake
And what of the snake
with his cold heart and cold-blooded veins?
At best a vixen should be a nuisance
At worst an enemy that needs to be dealt with swiftly and silently

The vixen questioned her feelings
yet could not help but fall under the snake's spell
His kills were magnificent
when his fangs of the finest pearl would sink into his victim's
        flesh with such finesse
she would shiver in pleasure at finally seeing a killer as eloquent
        as herself
As for the snake
he knew nothing of love
having neither received nor given it
yet he recognized a passion and life in the vixen's eyes not unlike
        his own
Thus, the snake found the affections of his killer beauty endearing
Against all-natural laws of God and Man, yes
but then again, no snake has ever cared enough to follow either's
        rule

One night the vixen entered her den
only to find the snake looking up at her from her bedding
As their eyes met, she slowly approached him
offering the vole she had caught for her dinner
A sacrifice for her love

Later, after the snake had accepted her gift, he curled his body
       around the vixen
whispering compliments and endearments to his lovely bedmate
She fell asleep knowing God's natural order was dead to her and
       her lover
He was gone when she woke up

On one particular day as the vixen was admiring her lover in his
       hollow
a hunter's bullet pierced her stomach
Her body twisted in agony
a macabre dance for her serpentine lover
Almost reverently the snake slithered up to her
curling his body around the vixen foolish enough to lose her heart
       to a snake
her snarl of pain became one of pleasure
as her lover sank his fangs into her throat

Better to be ended by her beloved's bite than a man's will

A Time for Worship

It's 4 o'clock in the morning
I glance at my love
 nude as the day of her birth

She is lying in her daddy's red pick-up truck
The air is heavy with the scent of sex, vanilla lotion, and fear
that her father will catch her making love to another girl

She is giggling
such a sweet sound
Her laughter puts cathedral bells to shame

I'm overcome with lust once again and begin to caress with my
          lips the woman I love
I refuse to not see her at the height of passion one last time
before the traitorous sun rises
separating me and my beloved once more

I memorize her form as if it is the last time
silken skin bronzed from the Texas heat
flaxen hair that tangles with mine when we kiss
the kindest green eyes in all the world

"No, we need to stop," she says half-seriously as I kiss her neck
and listen to her perfect cries for God
I will worship no other but her

Medusa's Mating Habits

We do not fit like puzzle pieces
Instead, our legs tangle like mating vipers
vulvas pressing together
arms coiled
green eyes reflecting each other as our bodies writhe
trying to reach something more while still staying together
Medusa herself would be proud
delighting in our Sapphic dance

As we lie together with nothing but the evidence of our lovers'
        play
my mind steals away to the Gorgon and the Goddess
Was it Medusa, Athena was jealous of, or Poseidon?
Perhaps she cursed Medusa with serpents to deflect from the
        confusion of her own feelings
Love contradicts Wisdom
It has no place in an intellectual's reasoning

And yet as I gaze into your eyes
seeing the reflection of everything that I am
I believe Medusa had the better deal
A lifetime of pretty mirrors
After all, who but a lover would gaze into the eyes of Death?

Heart

No one ever broke my heart
I froze it, you see
sealed it away in an icy tomb for all eternity
Neither fire nor ice picks could ever hope to warm or break it
Who would have fathomed that a single ray of sunshine would be
        enough
to unfreeze a heart that had vowed to never feel any lowly
        emotion?
Now I must learn to live with a heart that beats
and swim through seas of deception, pain, and melancholy
Love is certainly a bitch

Blue

That gorgeous, terrible hue which has haunted me beyond
        memory
has suddenly slammed its way back into my life
For years black has ruled my world
guarding and shaping me
For years I was able to forget that color which had betrayed me
And now, even though I have forsaken it
sneered at the unnamed emotion it represents for me
it has managed to cling onto me like a leech
draining the defenses and borders I have so ruthlessly put up
It is no coincidence that all of my lovers have had blue eyes
Only the ones who live in cerulean can appreciate the human
        experience
Love is flavorless without pain
And only in grief can we truly come to terms with its essence
When I first realized I loved you shocks of blue ran through my
        system
jolting me off my pedestal
my pretense of not being human, shattered
Now I must learn to live in blue once more

The Dance

It began with a note
My heart was lost as soon as I heard that melody
I took a step
Suddenly the ache of loneliness was gone
The trade of one world for another was made

The Dance became my life
A way to transcend the cruelties of my existence
At first, it owned solely my devotion
The rhythm of simply being was enough to sustain me
But I grew weary of not having a partner
I ached for phantom hands and lips to whisk me away into a
        haven
A place of pleasure with more passion and love than any in the
        world I had happily left behind

My lover was born from the delusions of a desperate soul
Unwilling to consider consequences
Thus, the Dance became a tango
A dark and twisted version of the reality I gave up
My phantom lover morphed throughout the years
Grey eyes became blue
The face changed but the purpose remained the same
To let me imitate living

Honestly, I would have happily been enslaved to my phantom
        lover until the day I died
But someone real cut in
She came out of nowhere
A glimpse of a slim and eloquent silhouette on an Indian
        summer's day
How was I to know that I met a tango thief that day
Suddenly it was her face gazing at mine
 Her face had replaced my phantom lover's
For the first time ever, I faltered in my steps
The Dance had changed

Love Baisant

Sometimes a girl just needs a hard fuck from the one she loves
We slam into the wall teeth bared like grinning Bobcats
There is nothing sweet about our union
No hesitation as we ruthlessly egg each other on
Forcing the other to prove their worth to our love
Your teeth sink into my neck as my nails maul your back
Like you, I want to draw blood
To mark and be marked
This isn't lovemaking; this is love fucking
Love Baisant
Let the romantics have their flowery sweet intimacies
Let them have their boyfriends and girlfriends
They don't have lovers
Lovers cannot be friends
Love is not candied
She is a masochist in all of her depraved glory
A possessive bitch with hot iron brands
There is no question between us whom the other belongs to
It is in your eyes which I wake up to every morning
It is in my gasps as you finger me in the shower before we go to
        work
We aren't romantics
Yet we are artists of romance
You bring me a thorny rose every Saturday
We do not imitate pendulums and call it dancing
Only tangos, salsas, and rumbas can satisfy our tastes in passion
We don't need breakfasts in bed or candlelit dinners
Let the romantics have their illusions and call them acts of love
Let the romantics have their friends that they call lovers
Let them have their lovemaking
Because as I gaze into the eyes that own my heart and soul
As we come down from heaven and back up from hell
I know there is no greater intimacy than to be fucked by my Love

Chopin's Ballade No. 2

My fingers gently caress the black and white keys.

A sweet melody floats around the room like a dove, gentle and
kind; a lover's dream.

Everything they tell us love should be, always relaxed, beautiful,
and happy.

Suddenly *he* is there, sliding behind me as my fingers abruptly
begin to dance erratically on the keys, the melody a
chaotic and passionate defiance.

His hands begin to play my body expertly.

There is no gentleness in the way he maps out my breasts,
stomach, hips, and inner thighs.

I don't make a sound as he slides my underwear down my legs.

He lifts me up as my fingers continue to produce moans and
screams of ecstasy on the abused black and white keys.

As we join neither of us says a word.

There is no need.

Chopin gave a voice to our lovemaking long ago.

My lover is not the prince charming I once dreamed of.

As my fingers and our lovemaking slow, I remember when the
dream for a prince became a reality.

I tried to be a good lover.

I wanted to enjoy my prince's gentle caresses; the tender, loving
endearments whispered in my ear as we made love.

But I couldn't.

At first, I thought there was something wrong with me because I
couldn't climax with soft lovemaking.

I didn't want to be treated as something fragile.

I wanted passion, to be the conquered as well as the conqueror.

I wanted to scream and sob and cause my lover to do the same.

I wanted to be ruined by love, to taste the double-edged sword of
both pain and pleasure.

So, I began to search beyond my prince's realm, convinced that I
had to settle for fucking to find any satisfaction in love.

Days were spent in passionate screwing.

Nights were spent in passionless shadows of lovemaking.

Years were wasted living in disgust, desperation, and self
-loathing.

Chopin was my savior.

His melodies offered the mixture of passion and tenderness that I
was convinced I would be deprived of forever.

It was through Chopin that I met *him.*

My dark angel, my lover.

I was in a bar, trolling for my latest conquest.

I suddenly heard Chopin's voice whisper to me from across the
room.

I glanced up at the piano, Chopin's favored choice of
communication.

Then, I saw his interpreter.

He was not the Grecian ideal of beauty.

He was dressed from head to toe in black, black shoes, black suit,
and a black hat.

The only thing of color on him was a ruby feather on his hat.

His skin was a dark, earthy brown.

His eyes were even darker.

If eyes are the windows to the soul his eyes were the windows to
Pan's.

His eyes promised all of Pan's erotic and impetuous nature.

Yet his eyes also held a familiar aspect, a tenderness I thought I
had seen in my prince's.

But these eyes held a thousand times more as they gazed into
mine.

If my prince beheld pearls when he gazed at me, this man beheld
gold.

After he was finished translating my Chopin, I followed him into
the alley out back.

We said nothing as our mouths collided, taking each other right
there on a chained fence.

It was not the fast fuck I was expecting, but a hard and slow
joining of two souls.

As those intense eyes gazed into mine, I finally found the balance
between fucking and lovemaking.

This fervent flight to Venus and Mars simultaneously was neither
and both.

It was the component of love in which stars had collided to make.
It was everything.
When it was done, I realized what I had done.
Complete and utter terror consumed me.
I realized that I had never been in love before.
Before my sultry gentleman could ask me my name I fled.
I fled as if all the legions of both hell and heaven were after me.
When I got back to my prince's castle, I shakily collapsed on our
        bed.
What had I done?
Why was it now that I realized I've never loved, and now that I
        finally did?
Overwhelmed I wept in relief.
Finally, I could give up this farce of a life I had starred in.
When my prince found me, I told him everything.
There was neither anger nor sadness in his gaze, just quiet
        acceptance.
And I knew.
This prince, this fantasy had never loved me.
He knew nothing of love.
He only knew what he was taught love should be.
That night I left his realm, my Cinderella act finally over.
I went back to the bar every night that week, waiting.
Then one night I heard it.
My Chopin's voice pure and loving, translated by Pan's soul.
As our eyes met once again, it felt like two souls were beholding
        mine.
        As we come down from our respected highs, I finish
        worshiping my glorious Chopin.
My lover, and oh the joy and sincerity I have to be able to use
        that word cradles me against his strong chest.
Our breaths are in perfect synchrony as I feel the comforting
        pulse of the only heart that will ever own mine.
I tilt my head and gaze into his warm eyes before I press my lips
        onto his.
In that soft flight to the cosmos, I whisper the name of the men I
        love.
Frederic.

Asexual Erotica

The moon gently bathes your skin in soft silver
Your beauty is truly the definition of sublime
Like Eve before her fall
Untarnished by sin and lust
We lay together, innocent
Eyes tethered
The occasional brushing of noses
Our lips do not steal kisses but rather share them
Love is pure and holy
There is no need to mar it with the sweaty, sticky violence of sex
Why would we want to profane our love with carnal desire?
Our bodies need not join, as our souls are already one
Let us lie forever chaste until the world ends in fire or ice by the
        hand of some god unknown
For you are the only warm flame and cool breeze I will ever need

Sax

The sexiest instrument on earth is the Saxophone
A golden erect cock spurting forth melodious vibrations
Every woman's dream
The dulcet sounds of that phallic wonder
Can give me either the most passionate fuck of my life
Or make the sweetest love I've ever cherished
I have a thing for voices
And by Satan does the Sax have a sexy one
Downright sinful screams of le petite mort
No wonder Blues musicians have sold their souls
For the privilege of stroking medallion keys to climax
If only ever I had a lover as passionate as a Sax
I too would gladly give up on the pipe dream of heaven for the
        tortures of hell
As long as that instrument of pleasure was burning alongside me
Voice drowning out the screams of fellow poor souls in perdition

See No Evil

I try not to stare
I try not to notice the robin egg blue and peach cream dress
Clinging tight to breasts and hips and bottom
I don't mean to violate her with my eyes
But how do you stop eyes from seeing?
I guess I could emulate Saul
Mutilate my eyes with sand
Use minuscule particles and molecules to make my eyes cloudy
and white and unappealing
A response to God's call for self-flagellation
But that won't stop my nose from inhaling lavender, violets, and
roses
Won't stop the tingling in my hand for soft smooth skin
Won't stop the longing in my lips for hers
So, I try not to stare
Lest my eyes reveal Saul's sins

Come Back to Me, My Michael

I miss you, Edith
How can I miss you when you are sleeping next to me?
You smell the same
honeysuckle intermingled with violets in a fragrant tendril
a tendril that used to include my own dandelion and wisteria
        scent
before you forsook me
forsook your blood
forsook your art
forsook your love
God's teeth Edith, you must know I miss him, too
I miss his fiery fur and brown eyes as compassionate as God's
but cutting yourself off from love, off from me, will not bring you
        any closer to either
Do you not remember our vow that April morning by the brook?
We swore before the God of Men and all the cosmos
that we would laugh, and love, and court Death himself
indifferent to men's laws and all the punishments of Heaven and
        Hell
We were reborn as a new entity
from that moment on we were known as Michael
and damn any other slanderous name they gave to us
Come back to me, My Darling, My Moonbeam, My Heart
Come back to me, and we will sing as we once did under the
        Aegean stars
indifferent and Immortal until the sky rains fire down around us
and we are united with our dear Hephaestus once more
Come back to me, My Heaven, My Hell, My Irresistible Sin
Come back to me, and we will make love until sun-up
when the Nightingales sing the last sleepy lullaby
as I kiss your lovely enraptured tears good morrow
Come back to me, My Michael, my Edith, My Love
Come back to me, and love me once more
For, I can never hope to love another
nor hope for my soul the ability to resist your fragile smile

Come back to me, and let us share our lives once more
Come back to me
Come back to me
Come back

Curves

The low-cut tank top reveals all
strong shoulder, black French lace brassiere, soft side, and the
      occasional tease of stomach
White gold curves peeking from behind a black field of eggshell
      sunflowers
A Hollywood starlet sashaying out of a film noir
I finally understand the meaning of tantalizing
for this is the sweetest torment
Fire surges and curves through my veins and I welcome the slow
      and fast burn

Seasonal

It was night when I almost hit you with my car.
I managed to stop an inch from you as my headlights hit your
        profile:
cropped brown hair, purple shirt, datolite eyes with small pupils
        like a cat's.
I jerked up my emergency brake so hard I nearly threw my arm
        out of the socket.

I kept seeing you on campus and at the grocery store.
A part of me thought I *had* hit you that night
and your ghost was trapped here on earth to haunt me.
My own personal demon.

We became acquaintances in the fall.
I thought I was the only one who liked to get high in the
        abandoned Walmart parking lot.
You and your boyfriend nonchalantly offered me a joint
as we sat and watched a Mexican woman across the street yelling
        puta at her daughter.

We became friends in the summer.
John broke up with you before leaving for New York.
You bitterly cried in my lap
my hands running through the now cropped rainbow hair

We fucked in the spring.
You were gay, and I knew you didn't suddenly start liking cunt.
I was a stone-cold sloppy second whose first and only time was
        against her will when she was high out of her mind.
Afterward, you mouthed at the needle scar and Chinese symbol
        for death on my inner thigh.

We made love in the winter.
You moved slowly in my ass
as I curled our legs and arms and torsos into an infinity sign.

We were fucked, but we were happy in our shared fuckedness.

It was day when you told me you walked in front of my car on
      purpose that night.
You weren't miserable with your life you simply didn't care.
I understood and told you I already knew.
Our kiss tasted like pot and the seasons, both of us quite content
      with the flavor.

To My Beloved Jane Shepard

The boldest thing I ever did
was snag your picture from the bulletin board
That isolated office was unworthy of your face
My first attempt to steal you away was unsuccessful
My usual cowardice prevented me
the same accursed thing that stopped me from kissing you that
    day
when we looked for your lost keys
and ended up rolling on the floor laughing when we found them
    hanging from your lock
My stupid heart lacked the courage
to lean down and dissect the mouth and feelings that had come
    to haunt my nightly thoughts
Why couldn't we be like Thelma and Louise
like Katherine and Edith
race into death happily rather than survive this existence apart?
So yes, I finally found the courage to lay claim to you
I was and still am too selfish to surrender my love to your
    knowledge
So, I remain content with kissing your paper face
rather than the lips, I know not, but miss none the less

Alaska

She thought living in Alaska would be romantic
like something out of those postcards that showed moose in the
        forest
or wolves hunting in the snow
She dreamt of hunting fowl and bears in the winter
bringing their skins and pelts home to her lover
Like a Neanderthal returning to her cave and mate

Instead, she delivers letters and packages
in the pitch-black dark at noon
Her gloves are tea stained
After her shift, she comes home to her lover Camille
She kisses Camille's brown cheek
dark as the tea she drinks every afternoon as she speeds through
        the snow
icy wind and frozen particles stinging against her cheeks

Camille was going to be a songwriter and singer
but the harsh climate strained her voice and passion
so, she ended up being a poetry teacher at the only high school in
        town instead

Camille wanted to move as far north from their small Georgia
        town as possible
Annie doesn't miss the scorching Georgia heat
nor the hot stares from their Christian neighbors
every time she and Camille walked down the street
To this day she doesn't know what they resented more
 that they were lesbians
that Camille was black, and she was white
or that she was ten years older than her then twenty-year-old
        lover

Annie takes off her tea-stained gloves and navy parka
She unties her plaid trapper hat, ruffling her cropped brown hair

      peppered with grey
She and Camille have lived two decades in Alaska
She sits on the scruffy armchair next to the crackling fire
listening to Camille read aloud the poem she's working on
Her third book comes out next winter
They haven't seen the sun for twenty-eight days now
Life is good